Underground with the Oriole

By Frank Lima

Inventory (Tibor De Nagy Editions)

Frank Lima

Underground with the Oriole

E. P. Dutton & Co., Inc. | New York | 1971

PS
3562
.I46
U5

Copyright © 1971, 1970, 1968, 1967, 1963, 1962, by Frank Lima
All rights reserved. Printed in the U.S.A.
First Edition

No part of this publication may be reproduced or
transmitted in any form or by any means, electronic
or mechanical, including photocopy, recording, or any
information storage or retrieval system now known
or to be invented, without permission in writing
from the publisher, except by a reviewer who wishes
to quote brief passages in connection with a review
for inclusion in a newspaper, magazine, or broadcast.

Published simultaneously in Canada
by Clarke, Irwin & Company Limited, Toronto and Vancouver

Library of Congress Catalog Card Number: 70-133596

SBN: 0-525-22590-0 (cloth)   SBN: 0-525-04650-X (paper)

The author wishes to thank the editors of the following
publications, in which his poems have appeared:
Adventures in Poetry: "Underground With the Oriole," "'Salad Exit,"
"February '68," "Harbor," "Demitasse," "prospero";
Art and Literature: "The Welder"; *C:* "The Woman"; *Evergreen
Review:* "Pudgy," "Hotel Park"; *Mother:* "Acid"; *Paris Review:*
"News," "Penicillin," "Submarine"; *Provincetown Review:*
"Inventory"; *Signal:* "Abuela's Wake"; *The Wagner College
Literary Review; The World:* "Ode to Love"

To Kenneth Koch

Contents

Inventory—To 100th Street   11
Mulatta   14
Hotel Park (East 110th St.)   16
Mom I'm all screwed up   17
Primavera   19
Abuela's Wake   20
Pudgy   22
Gorilla   25
Empty Cage   27
Poem   28
Poem   29
Tuesday   30
Shoe   31
Poem   32
Beach   33
Haiku   34
The Woman   35
The Welder   37
Filter   40
The Ruin   41
Submarine   42
Myrrh   43
Spanish Poetry   44
Penicillin   45
Acid   46
Harbor   47
Voices   48
Sombra   50
News   51
Purple   52
Lime   53

Ventriloquist   54
Poem   55
Poem   56
Underground with the Oriole   57
Demitasse   59
February '68   60
sky—   61
Land of a Thousand Dances   62
Scorpio Rising—   64
summer (a love poem)   65
Salad Exit   67
strawberry (a love poem)   69
prospero   73
capricorn   75
Ode to Love   78
Ode to Love—Part 2   80
yellow   83
canto   84
sara   85
june sara   86
my life   87
river sara   88
morning sara   90

"My world is another one than the one
I have to accept. Therefore from time to time, I have to lie
to preserve this world of mine.
I wish I would not have to lie to anyone."

Picasso

Inventory—To 100th Street

For John Bernard Myers

In the corner lot
  where they parked
        green banana trucks
    fruits
        palmed in paper straw
I smell
     bedbug & kitchen-cockroach
         summer afternoons

Somewhere
     tailless
       one-eyed cats
    doting in fat garbage cans
       screaming with the stench
  of rice & beans
        strawberry tampax
    piled
      high as the smell
        (I was small & slick)
  the covers tilted
      like the hat of a rock-look wino
      in a deep
         knee-bend nod
    on a beer
        can-street
          Sunday morning

There were always
     time-thick
       empty nights
  of nothing to do

                        but listen to the
            ethereal
                    (she lived on the top floor)
            I-go-for-more screams
                    of Charlie pimp's woman
                            when he beat her
                    for his good
                            business principles
                    joy-pop the block
                            with morning-talk

I hear the dim iron dawn yawning
                    (I lived on Third Ave.)
    rattle
        nights into
                Saturday morning
        flag-bloomer
                eclipses
    just before the hunt—
            they were as big—
            the cats
    like jungle bunnies
        fierce with fleas & sores

I see window-people
    hanging out of gooey-stick slips
                sweating
                strange
    below-the-button drawers
            crouched junkies in hallways
                with monkey backs

12

            eating cellophane bananas
                    on a g-string
                            waiting
                    for that last bust
            Spics with cock-comb
                            hair fronts
                    ear-gulping mambo music
                    eye-lapping pepperican flower
                            crotches

I can hear the streets whispering
                    in the ears of yelping kids

            in the fun-gushing that
                    rippled my blood
                            in the pump

                            but the kids
                                    are dying in the lot
                            like the tarry-blown feet
                                    of the rain
                                            jingling
                            on the rusty-green
                                    of yesterday's
                                            fire escapes.

Mulatta

To Phyllis

And if I love you, we'll fight.
   I'll call you bitch, tack head,
And curse the gods, Lincoln, and the feminists.
Beat you—not too hard, in the right places—
   Stuff, I'm a man, no trick!
Laugh, when you cry like a child, hurt . . .
Bite, swallow the lump in my throat.
Leave,
   Take the money,
Get my belly full of cheap gin & beer;
Head full of good smoke next to a
Greasy, grinny, lipstick whore with
   Endless, sympathetic: hum-hum, definitely,
   You're right, baby—
   In the mist of reefer,
Cigarette and stale-green cigars,
In a bar gray with the laughter of
   Hustlers, junkies, and steady, stink-finger tricks
   Where the scream of the jukebox
Swells the air and makes my brain thick
   With forget-you
   And then,
The scent of your hair, body,
   When you finished cleaning the house—
      I found it so delightfully unpleasant,
Sends the blood screaming through my legs for you,
And explodes the tingling blue bubble I'm in . . .
Homesickness of you begins to seep in,
   Slowly, cruelly till night skulks away
From sour, headachey dawn.
   And if I love you,

I'll wait and beat the ancient seconds of
    Without-you-since-yesterday,
As I stumble, back-bent, fumbling for keys,
Chewing Juicy Fruit,
    Up the squeaky stair, just to drown you,
    Just once more,
    In an ocean of fresh new
    I'm sorries—baby—darling—honey—please—
    And hungry, stale-smoke-liquor kisses,
Gaudy, alien perfumed hugs.
And if I love you, the bitch storm
Passes to the crisp white lap of
    Sheets and pillows,
Where I wander in—up—out—down
    The chesnut thighbone avenue,
Barely touching, panting, my nostrils
    Blowing
On your softsilk body to mine,
A cherry-nostrum wonder—
Experience . . .
              BANG!
. . . And if I love you, we'll fight again.

Hotel Park (East 110th St.)

My fingers
        popping with eyes
            touch you
    in a sea of foaming sheets

I beauty-mark your blubbery thighs
        mash thick kisses
            on your swollen lips
                your tongue puddles in my ear
    I'm king of the ceiling

The bed beehives with sighs
        my nose spiders
           in your mouse-tit hair
            babybottle breasts
        dance with the springs
    your meshy bush
            drips with nightdew
                nailed to my loins
                like religion

Then grisly seconds clog
        the sand-clocks
    love's funk hangs
        in the room
            like a dirty shirt
we leave
        but life pools behind
            the hairy socket
                it smells like a miracle

    we're sixteen.

Mom I'm all screwed up

Moth-eyed
    by the neon sign
        I peeped
          at the stiff little worms
            screwing in your head
           spider crabs
              crawled in my ear

With popping antennae ringlets
    you looked like
        a preying mantis
          cold cream & turban
            science fiction gleam
        as real
    as cancer
      spreading
          stuffed-tits-and-rag-guts
            yawning
              brillo-crotch
              that stunk
                all over me
        playing
          Johnny-on-the-pony
              on me
                    indoors

The mattress groaned
        I moaned
     Mom
         I'm no horse
              you have pimples on your butt

                    your belly button droops
                        your boy pop left
                            the rose of your hopes
                                no
                                    no

With lollipop-grin lips
        on my solitaire piece
            you had no teeth
                I'm still scaling scabs of
                    hot garlic
                            slob-kisses

    isn't mamacita's heart going to
                kiss mom
                        good night
                            no
                                no
                                    no.

Primavera

      A mummy
         crumbling
            in the bar

my eyes
   empty mirrors
        my kidneys
            drunken flowers

   Then dawn
      an eyelid

                I come to you
                  as always
  green
     tired
        need a shave
           a bath
       I stink
unlock the nights
    in jail
  it's spring on the windows
my heart
  in a bag
    and some beer

           Hi Monkey
           I'm home

Abuela's Wake

Then her mouth flew open
    like a fish sucking air
        Jesus flipped with a greasy hook
    I wanted to pop a cap in his plaster head

Abuelo laid with her
        naked
    he blew his nose
    his eyes
        broken toys
  while he sang her to sleep

                I'll tie your cold finger with
                ribbons for the wedding ring—
                I sold your teeth when I was drunk
                Negra Bird-Lips   my heart   your grave . . .

His lips fumbled on her wrinkled breasts
    Mom screamed barbed wire
        in my shoe-high ears
my stickball smile fell off my face

Concha
    the wake's witch
        wearing her mothball smile
           held the black rosary
              like a snake with a Catholic head
                  it still hisses in my bed
        dribbling the wooden words

Dios te salve Maria
Dios te salve Maria

outside
   the mouth of December shit on the windows

By the stumped candles
   ice-bird white tearing wax
     Abuelo pillowed her head
       in the mouse-velvet coffin
         smeared her chalk face with
          glass kisses & drunken tears
the wreaths were shadows
     standing in the corners

Abuelo sits in the kitchen
   Abuela's eyes are berries in his head
     he drinks her face in Gallo wine
       it licks his heart
         by the wedding picture
     in the empty bedroom

Abuelo
     her eyes are pools the rain can't find
      she sleeps in a green gown of moss
       and tiny paws of dew dress the grave

    your heart's a tin cup
       begging for wine.

Pudgy

I'd swish through the door
    tiptoeing
        goofed on speedballs
            with a yellow-jaundice twinkle
            in my glassy eyes

      you'd be waiting in the kitchen
        perched on a chair
          like Judge Leibowitz
          your face mooned
            wet thighs
              at me

Instead
    I'd stash my joints
        in the food-bare freezer
          take five
            throw off my clothes
          drop in bed
              like an empty pebble

I'd stink of
        catting on roofs & in basements
        barnacled with sores & pimples
            sweat-starchy socks & greasy underwear
            on my back two weeks
    you looking top-flight
      curlicues of perfume
        running through your nesty hair
but I was slimming-off
        in sleep

a glazed tear on your chubby cheek
   whimpering out
               *I found a bag of that stuff
               in the Bible—
               You're never home anymore*
    aaahhh
           shut up—
                  you're lucky I'm home tonight

and nod back in my bucket
   till the monkey
      creaked my back awake—
         gobble out of bed
            fireman my clothes on
               pistoled out of the house
after I'd beat you out of your
   carfare & lunch money
      for my morning fix

I took cures & cures
   wrote you letters

               we'll start all over
                  never take off again
                     clean up for good this trip
                     you were my first high
                        cop a slave & work for you only
                     I'm really getting down in therapy
                                       this time

                  sign them

       Your forever
       Loving husband

     P.S. I need commissary

  on a paper napkin
    you wrote
      Dear Liar
        Come home.

O my chocolate princess
   I lay in bed
    smelling of Lifebuoy soap & toothpaste
   light a stogie & watch the smoke
   unshoe ghost-nude thoughts

     my feet gag my heart
        they're cold.

Gorilla

To 1959

        Eyes tearing
           nose running
      then the yawn
       and his head
        a wreath of ice
with a handful
        of raisins for hair
    razors & twitches
   in his joints
    keep him from
      the floor
   to the cot
     and his eyelids
    blink like hammers
The cramps in his stomach
    double up to his knees
      he yawns
    and his ribs stick out
      like thorns
              Call for the hack
               he's dying
"Tell him to drink cold
water and walk slow"
                  the heartbeats hang on the bars
                    and fall through the tier
                      like sunlight

Ice him—
  let him take to the sheets
  and dance with the bulb
            "Save it for Sunday and
            let them pass the plate"

         The catnaps
              glassine dreams
                   of golden cookers
                   dollar bill collars
     hypos—
          like glass hummingbirds
              in his arm
              turn to wood
     he yawns
       blows his fix
       he's awake
and the shadow of the hack
       hangs upside down.

Empty Cage

    I've been looking at the
        old question mark

    It screams
        while I sleep
        whispers
        when I walk

It kills
    eats
        and vomits everything

    I want to see
        water-colored
            walls
        in the Tombs

        a suede-top nigger
            running for
                president
                    not trees.

Poem

My brother
    fixed his new
      cuff link
  to ride the lightning
    for murder
  and Mom ironed
    his clothes
  for summer camp

        You know how
        fussy he is

this morning smelled
  like burned hair

Poem
    To My Father

Iron
Iron

I
Have
Burned
Down
The
Sky.

Tuesday

My heart is a
    grasshopper
  between your breasts
    the bedsheets are winter
      we cling to each other
the walls are on fire

My nose is in your ribs
    your lips in my hair
      the moon
        a red lip-print
          in your navel
  and your legs
    two black highways
      around my neck

Your eyes are filled
  with ponies & stars
    your body
  a carnival flower
    where naked nuns
    crawled in my ear
    crowned with pin drops
      of sweat
  dance in my head

Shoe

      May these
      roses keep
      the secret
      when I hold
             You
there's an
old lamp
      burning
  up
    side
       down
            in my heart
  O my Love
  the fumes
  go to my head

I prefer
 your
    toe.

Poem

    The carnival is
        knocking at
          the door
          to pluck
          the flowers
          in my
                heart

Shoe

      May these
      roses keep
      the secret
      when I hold
            You
there's an
old lamp
      burning
  up
    side
        down
            in my heart
O my Love
the fumes
go to my head

I prefer
 your
    toe.

Poem

The carnival is
   knocking at
     the door
     to pluck
     the flowers
     in my
          heart

Beach

There
   happy as a greenfly
     toes popping out
       like corks in the sand
         Buddhas on stilted chairs
           ocean tattooed with
              bathing caps
          mud castles
              seashell windows
           and sunglasses staring
                at the panty-blue sky
webbed seaweed
      windblown
 brown
         on an eel-green
                bottle

On the meat line
   sun sprays of iodine
      on fish-white backs
         wide splits
            heavy squats with cat whiskers
I'm the ocean between their legs
      my toetips cling to the seashore
         sea gulls whirlpool in my hair
            and sing in my windy ear
O Beach
   heaven of dark-eyed belly buttons
      you tricked-off the seashell
         for Trojan-floats & beer cans.

Haiku

For Frank O'Hara

I
The lights are out
The cats are hungry
The room is full of gangsters

II
The dishes are dirty
The icebox is empty
I dream of celery and a compass

III
The roof is upstairs
The window next door
A guitar in the shower

IV
The hours disappear in my room
Where is my blue pistol
The door-god is knocking.

The Woman

Today I met my woman in the subway . . . it was winter.
She wore a red coat down to her knees with a black
fur collar. I could only see the back of her head,
which was blue because of the kerchief & the flower
she wore. She wasn't facing me. Her shoes were
orange and her stockings black. I went up to her
and said I had found a little part of her in all
the women I had ever known, and I had always loved her.
I told her: "We can make it & crib together . . .
things won't be too bad . . . life is a snap!"

Then she turned to me. Her face was sea-brown; her
lips were thick; her eyes were dried wells and the
flower in her hair was plastic. I said to her that
I loved her more than ever now and must know her name
because she was what life was about. She grinned:
her teeth were stubs of jade. I kissed her and sucked
her lips. She said any name would do. . . . I called her
My Woman and I took her hand. It was like old dried
wood with cracks in it; her knuckles were cold lumps
I pressed to my face.

She unbottoned her coat. Her body was black and her skin
was wrinkled and stuck to her bones like tape. She had
no breasts; they were eaten away by cancer I guess.
My hands were filled with warm and slippery flesh.

She kicked off her orange shoes and asked me to kiss
her feet . . . they were small and her toes were chewed
stubs. I said I would kiss them if only she would give
me her heart. She said she would in exchange for mine.

I told her my heart was young and full, filled with flowers, birds and perfumed tears, but if she wanted it she could have it.

The train came to a sudden stop. It was spring. I fell away from her across the aisle dreaming of wreaths. She dropped her heart and kicked it over to me. I took it . . . it was a coffin filled with dry worms. I ran off with it, as happy as a faggot in boy's town.

The Welder

To David Smith

I
He is gliding on her like a block of ice
On an iron stove

I am from a distant land

He gave her a brick
Cut off her hair
It is falling
She is sinking

I have walked in front of buildings
Put your hand in the sunlight on the maps
Your head in the river
We will live in the sea
Or your hair

Falling
Your lips are red like snow
Indian head   Orizaba   Mexican beer

II
She is leaning like a Russian bird
The early smells
Surrounding like landslides
Her fingers skating near my arm
I am gliding

I once lived in Havana

III
A thin lamp in my hand
A scrim

The third act is a shadow crossing a child
They are glass
The clown is in love with the lock
On her wrist

She is rushing against my hands
The flowers are sinking in the room like ether

IV
Our bodies are fish trembling in gelatine

I turn my waist
A machine
To the tip of your cheek
A circus

I am living in your stockings
Volcanoes

V
A green cigarette
A purple mouth
A factory
Quick
   Safar

VI
My hands are surrounding
Your calendar
A sunflower
One foot across

I turn my waist
A green cigarette

The sea is sinking
With figures in her hair
A purple factory of lead suns
On your cheek

The sharks are melting in
The snow like volcanoes

A glacier suffocating a siren.

Filter

Her legs began in the sky
She moved away slowly like a coat in a dream
I camouflaged her face and we moved through stones
Through long luminous arms—
The string on the window is a funeral in the desert
A photograph in a volcano   A silk mouth on a glass
She is winding around my waist   A factory of blue air
The sun rises like a kerosene star on my nail
The tide snaps on the glass floor
We accumulate in the dark and dissolve in the air.

The Ruin

For Mike Goldberg

Because the colors are extravagant and so intense
As I rise to the surface moving toward the great light
Watching the sand rotate with the gypsum in the heat—

Each day the sun beats me in some dry place
Forcing me to run away and find the shade
I sit and hide from the damp stars
Knowing that they do not last
Symbols of my long body

I cannot poison the entire earth
Bringing terrible trembling to an obscure arm or foot
Because of moisture and sound suddenly beautiful
I am alone in my crust watching the sea in a dream
I am alone watching the sky I have no dignity in the air

The vultures are spinning like wild birds
Waiting for dust and incense
I fan the sand the source of my universe
Separating the forming appearance between us
—The smell and the feathers—
I move noticing the glimmers
And eat my dream of sand the color of your flesh.

Submarine

I cannot feel her voice I am too far away skiing in Austria.
Perhaps I will go to another country disguised as frozen gas
And travel beneath her skirt into the center of the earth.
I have an air bubble in my ear that needs light.
It is yellow and I slip over the lintel to correct the sun.

Here is a white charm. My hand cannot hold it.
The stars are lost and the birds have absorbed the wind.
It doesn't matter I am going mad listening to the noises—
The young girls on the waves. They are white like telephones.
My arms are tired and they will not let me go because I refuse
To undress them without passionate words.

Myrrh

The light has moved across her long back like a soft sound
And I live off the effects twisted in strings
I know what marble we are going to soak
And where the colors stay intact
When the sand flies and mixes against her body
Like a flurry of pearls on solid blood
My arms begin to bend the water and lashes fall on the banks
There are traces of dew on her neck and I lie on the rocks
torn by the weather   The ground still moves in a song
Though at a whisper.

Spanish Poetry

There is nothing left but a change in the room
And you are changing with it like the voices in the next room

You emerge like towers into the smoke
With uncompromising love dipped into water
Then there is nothing left
But the sentries on the walls

What are we building today?
Perhaps something of importance
Because I have raced through the wind to find the end
Your life's stories have no consequence on the earth
It is much too small where you are

This is not the end in your case
Because you are one of the people who will remain for some
    time
You will meet Valentino and lay yourself by his clay feet
And wipe his tears with your white wings.

Penicillin

To Harold Krieger

Here I am born a brilliant mistake from infinity
And the idea of existence reminds me of turtles
December is the day of insects in bloom for horoscopes
The duty of love is hiding a corner of flesh
A hot mouth with beautiful teeth

The earth is familiar to me small and beautiful
Like a cup of coffee a running joke in the mornings

I am breathless in this mad race with the butterflies
They encircle my head and choke the air in my chest
To remind me of my body when it snows on fingertips

What becomes of a poet with a common cold? Nothing.
I want to own the air and glitter in a hot shower
Because I have copied everything I have seen.

Acid

      through a hole in my hand
         I have your face in my hand
I have a knife on the ceiling
To fly through the ceiling
Like a knife in your room
I kill the walls in your room
While the dead women sleep
We smoke through the walls
We inhale the walls
Our bodies are beautiful
They are numbers in our throats.

Harbor

I have counted the chemicals for a hundred reasons
For some trick to shift my vision
From the half constructions of one to another
We wander in catastrophy like needles in the air
Singing of fire

We lie in twos threes and fours
We think like diamonds in a glove
And listen to the stir as we fly toward each other
As though thoughts were planets against reason and cold

She lies in her own periphery like a soft lake
In the circle I touch her eyelids with a blow
And watch her perish
Like an utter kiss.

Voices

September '66

I am standing on the warm earth
The yellow fist revolves around me
Uncoiling the windows
I wipe them with metal and watch them dry like the waves

We are in a restaurant dreaming of a bed of grape leaves
Blood is curling on a glass to test the air
The sun is sealed in front of the rug
Listening to our breathing as it slides off us
Into frozen signals

Voices are covering the green air
As we rise toward the buildings
Avoiding the pleasures of a foxhole
To keep the whispers from the clouds

No! The slaves are playing for us
I have iron legs against you
You are down on the earth
Spread like a fan on the sea paralyzing the wind

The cymbals are stumbling behind me
Because I'm drunk and everything seems deliberate
Like snow and dirty pearls
Cover the ice cubes with bourbon to stop the infection
Pretend it is a cluster of flowers
I am swooning and the room is spinning

I see the summer by the church
I hate the man who cut my ear

I heard the sound and turned
And left him without a hand—

The river Oka is dark and hot where the great pike
Travels through aluminum skin on your thin shoulders
Below me you will float on a sheet of silver
And I will drown in the snow like a pair of boots
Because I love you and the air is hard in the bright sky.

Sombra

Her name is ice with accordion lips
Undressing a lake in my face
        Her skin is yellow
My hands are listless on her face
        We swallow   I stab her
The maps make blood
        Our tongues roll
The world is flat
        Two fish smell
The sun freezes the hurricane in my throat
You are beautiful on the bus with your legs
        Around my neck
               like two owls
        With one leg
I am an elevator falling through my hands
        Your mouth is on the walls
        We are lovers in a glass
My fingers are sand
        The windows are flying
        I blow smoke around your ear
Put flutes in your hair
        O my beautiful ceiling
        She is sleeping on the rug
With a knife in her head.

News

For Tony and Irma Towle

Today I am in the room watching the sun evaporate.
I recognize *Bathsheba* almost perfectly preserved
In turquoise and jade. Above, it has fangs and a
Field of human teeth the color of red lacquer with a thin
Mouth of green patina.

The islands are still obscure like iron eyes on the
Surface of the sea. On the left, a woman, the triangular
Type gently swelling over the figure of a man. It is Venice,
The city of beautiful cows and gentle rains of dull maroon.
This remarkable head of Man once belonged to a mortuary in
Oran. He was buried so his ideas might be better known.

There are women in the snow with different colors in their hair.
They float through my vision much greater than the sky.
Their lines remind me of the seashore and the reflections
In the rocks, like smoke and ash in a dream. We must never
Become so involved; I am eleven inches high and I can lose
You in a photograph like a rope dancer.

Glucose and sodium bicarbonate: A flowing river after a hang-
    over.
My head is set in motion, my arms begin to move and I can hear
It must be the day of judgment, the alarm clock has stopped!
I want to be in South America where there is no water to make
Alcohol. My apartment is a jungle. Nothing must move.
We have five seconds to die. I will collapse instead, like spring.

Purple

There is an orange tree
Breathing in the room—

She is lying transparent
The bed is encircling her
Like swimmers . . .
The blood is settling in
Every inch of the statue
In half whispers
A shoulder emerges from the sediment
A thin sunny wrist

I'll lure her on the gray ice
Distributing myself among distant dancers

It is beautiful
The scattering of our lungs
The iron crab
Returning to its wings
Underwater near the sea
In order to be imitated.

Lime

The secret voyage goes through my mind like distilled ruins
I hold the rain in my hands waiting for the figures to pass
When it is done there will be rain in the east
The provinces will be late with warm evenings   dunes
And clear green skys   And if I die the seals will cross
    the air
And fall behind the ocean and desert.

Ventriloquist

To Virgil Thomson

I can listen to all the sounds from my window
They are three feet wide and four feet high
There is no jealousy in a compass
My breath is eleven colors.

Poem

Tomorrow
I'll go
Fishing
On the
Ganges
With an
Orange
Some rice
And gather
My hands
Then I'll
Entreat
Your window
On a scaffold
In September
I'll hide
In your
Shower
Because
I am also
A philosopher

Poem

There
Is an
Earth
Quake
In the
Next
Room

I will
Mail
Her a
Picture
Of my
Hand

She
Will
Send
Me a
Light
House.

Underground with the Oriole

To Joe and Rosemary

I have been bled
Twice this year . .
But I can see the workers,
They are like stones that keep the sky in place.
The weather is like the sky,
The arch of heaven with incredible weight,
With a blue curve that does not let me sleep.

Below us the bathers wade in rings of water:
And it is April as we leave the room with a glass of music,
Judging my footsteps carefully.
The soles of my feet are Greece,
And I have a beautiful wind.

The oil in the sand reminds me of paradise.
I wish I were underground with the oriole:
I would wear a bronze mask and give you my silver,
My accounts and my green vestments
So no one would pass or hesitate at your figure,
The figure of a sea horse.

In the air lovers are whispering to each other,
They believe in mirages and paper formulas.
In Asia the dispute for ashes has begun:
The itchy substance for allegory
Where the stones lie by the water in a trance.
I have been here seven years pretending
To go mad on a bed of fire,
But the rains are imminent this year.

It is Sunday in the huge glass house
As we descend the stairs to lay the flowers by the sea—
Suddenly the man with the watch is overwhelmed,
By the fog,
It was beautiful the clear silhouette of her body
In the deserted streets,
As though the atmosphere had lost its way
In the frantic upheaval of the crowds.

My skin has grown tighter from the strain,
I'm no longer in radiant health,
There is an epidemic raging in me:
I am afraid of birds.
A cold blast of air has hit my stomach!
Was it an earthquake?   Or an approaching storm?

The crossing was very difficult.
The light was pink on the foam of the crashing waves.
They glowed like coils with ruffles on the edges.
On the bottom the seaweed moved carefully
In a desert on a soft night
As the moon turned toward the wall.

I came away from the crowd seasick:
Each summer I have lost a wife in this room—
I tighten the bed with winter and prepare for disease
And rub my body with alum and water
Knowing I will drown in the undercurrent
With the forms on the ceiling and the ladder pointing
Toward the window.

Demitasse

For Patsy Southgate

Suddenly I am awake in the great zoo
and fighting for my life in the darkness
for love. I will save myself and electrocute
the cat. The soft pain is on the butcher's block.
Dinner is a terrible thing when you think of
no rain for broccoli and asparagus and the love sick
animal we are having for dinner in wine sauce.
We will fight for the last morsel because we are
wonderful guests and prodigies of our stomachs
and that pink tropical foliage the salad you
tossed out the window. It is five o'clock in the
morning and time for demitasse and a swim in the pool
because we have crossed the Alps and hamburgers are great!

February '68

My dreams haunt me:
I wear my watch to bed
Because I cannot sleep alone.
I honor my arms because they have held you.
I am a ghost when I dream and answer
The phone like a dwarf. Even at my best
I am a helicopter when I write to you across
The ocean. I put your hair away in the morning
When I dream of you so no one will find it,
In the event someone breaks in.

I have bought a gun to guard your letters.
I have spread green powder on your paintings
So no one will touch them. I have undermined
The apartment with your presence and foolish
Arguments to keep myself from becoming uncivilized.
I have been asked to make a speech about the hole
I burned in my pajamas when I read your last letter.
I tested the weather and went for a swim.
I, an island, with winds and trees, loves you.
It's true, I'm surrounded by water and I will die
Because of the distance that separates us, but I
Will come to you across the ocean like a great spider.

sky—
    sara

although the sky is soft
and I am in love with
the rim of the world

I think of your walk
and I will say to you
how I love you
and the wind from
your cigarette

I will touch your hands
and they will dream
of what we are
and they will wait
for us like the wind
between them

a flame runs over us
and we grow larger than the sky
and we are lost in an idea
and I shall tell you of my life
and of the fires that touch me
each afternoon

                                          nov. 15/69

Land of a Thousand Dances

There are no stars tonight Lilly Lips
just your body a long Turkish urn
I shined and filled at night an adjustment I made once a week
pretending to be an artificial Earth

I gave myself to the nudist colony across the street
after jumping up and down for days
I would sink into the rug like a submarine
as you watched television like a snow body

The properties of love are simple:

1. Fuck.
2. Fuck.
3. Fuck.

You lack one of these . . . you are a symptom I've removed
from my life a feeling and sometimes a memory when
I turn on the lights in my room a tradition in my dreams
a microscopic slogan of the twentieth century

My love poems to you are apparitions that got lost in the
wind out there somewhere   O you ruined my suit too
as I brought you back from the dead to write you waves
locks and tendons invisible as I am I feel famine
I want to zone you O Europe the creep's continent of dull art:

Unfailfull?   Never!   I always thought of you
                                        and this island another
                                        harsh body of water

No the world is not that round and I will see you face
    to face and
set you on fire and you will melt so here is an herb for
    your salty
teeth!

The scorpion cuts my sleep in half when I am naked with my
trembling heart among a crowd that meets me halfway down
the corridor with dried bread: We do not eat fish we are fish

O my parable I sleep with myself like an ocean empty
of fish death and reflections and if they take my sleep away
you will give it back to me when you return from
the sky like a forest fire for one last moment with you
on the North Pole because I'm the favorite spot of the
    leopard!

                                    sunday, feb. 9/69

Scorpio Rising—

I am standing still I am an old man I am the middle of the sea
in a teaspoon O your beautiful lungs it's too bad I can't
live on land but watch the tides I wrest away the worlds
I bring to you with my big finger to the hush of lava
and whispering arms like the furious lizard in the sun
we dive into a kiss as once a thumb was born to the Mississippi
river sliding down your skirt like a great dorsal and this
weather and its islands are a white machine in my head
as the stars float on top of us and crush the boredom!

may 8/69

summer   (a love poem)

I wanted to be sure this was our island
so we could walk between the long stars by the sea
though your hips are slight and caught in the air
like a moth at the end of a river around my arms
I am unable to understand the sun your dizzy spells
when you form a hand around me on the sand

I offer you my terrible sanity
the eternal voice that keeps me from reaching you
though we are close to each other every autumn
I feel the desperation of a giant freezing in cement
when I touch the door you're pressed against
the color of your letter that reminds me of flamingos

isn't that what you mean?
the pleasure of hands and
lips wetter than the ocean
or the brilliant pain of
breathless teeth in a
turbulent dream on a roof
while I thought of nothing
else except you against
the sky as I unfolded you
like my very life a liquid
signal of enormous love we
invented like a comet that
splits the air between us!

the earth looks shiny wrapped in steam and ermine
tired of us perspiring at every chance on the floor
below I bring you an ash tray out of love for the

ice palace because it is the end of summer the end
of the sun because you are in season like a blue
rug you are my favorite violin when you sit and
peel my eyes with your great surfaces seem intimate
when we merely touch the thread of life and kiss

july 30/69

Salad Exit

I am in love and irritable on this island!
We are in this great city waiting for fresh stars
Artisans of simple life, of images and laws of boredom.

      "Should we build a concert of snow?
      For an art the lowest chaos
      The immense dealings of a future ruin?"

I cannot speak to you and wait for humidity my brilliant shield
We are one world a system in a garden a prosperous tube
Cool overnight and maybe a blanket.

O my favorite fever anything I might say is a continent
As if you were a salamander you wander around the flames
And breathe light a hundred ways should you pretend to be a
      woman
How little you know of my sleep in the narrow green leaves . . .
The drops run like starfish.

There is a flaw in the air beneath my finger
You are an almond I dip into to see all things
An enormous flowing zodiac in a yellow cup of docile hair.

      ". . . There is a shadow in my arms
      ignorant of my moving blood insisting
      I am not dead."

    The world is a sweating bitch
    A salad exit of sweet hair
    A trapeze tattoo

A corpulent misdemeanor on my index finger
An eyelash on my stinkin' cock!

The overtime of motion is a pigeon's dream . . .
Like repetitious hair freezes on a swollen trap whose
    body is a rail
So we are giants unwashed and probing as we serenade a dime
    on the
Floor to level off a dive and clean the sky with harmony

        O my city hand tomorrow is East!

                june 4/69

strawberry   (a love poem)

"... you are my sunshine ..."

1
the articles in these lines
are gentle like an orange
that has struck some bright
fabric
                but
you are not ready
for the only worth
the tremors and regrets

it is to be learned
one who wishes
is the souvenir of logic
the legend in the room
the perfect cry in the universe
like
                a radio

complete with laws
and discipline at the
bottom of the atlantic
which has nothing to
do with my life

2
yet I will lead you
by the hand back to
earth and love you
like the floor you
are liable to melt
over the grandness

of space
          invisible
and white
the air I stumble
on the rooftops
and orbit with such
a sound of laughter

my thoughts mingle on your
northern face the delicate
inheritance of your hair
I cannot see my
          hands
dry in this lucid
place   like trophies
in the equinox

3
when we breathe
flesh and air are near us
no wonder the room is never
there when you
look up
          suddenly
over my glass
shoulder . . .   I repave my streets
in the middle
of the night
and slip into
your fur coat

        for the sake of first aid
          . . . a Chinese dinner

waiting for you
to come once to
an agreement of parts
the root of all
things   acceptable

4
I believe in the energy of the grand style
in   strawberry   yogurt   love   love
because I am wearing a white summer shirt
with parallel lines that remind

          me   of   you

      "there is a parking meter in my nose
      it is in love with my sinus
      it needs an aspirin and some sun . . ."

a poem I wrote you yesterday
you were nervous I felt great
I ignored your condition on the sofa
so I'm different in this weather
and better in the winter am I you

      ". . . you are my sunshine . . ."

anyhow

5
there is tremendous self
confidence in my typewriter
and I don't mean lead

I have lived on this island
thirteen months I can't control
myself
                some
one has written
your name on the trees
when you get a chance
walk around my island
you will find some other
footprints of other robinson
crusoe's

on the other hand
it's dawn since I'm
not in bed . . .
                she's jumped
in my lap to
tell me we have a life
together even though
I only have two
feet among the relics
my vices intrusions equally
naked come what may

                                      july 4/69

prospero

there is a fire on the moon
because my blood dreams of salt

it glides and divides the earth
sanctioning my infancy
partial and insignificant
like an iron fence basking
in the sun

each day I smoke more and more
and invent my own skills
I can image a poster of snow
and dates as my hands twist
this glass a crucial sign of
my sanity in attendance
a dignified worm circling
my head altering
my echo beyond salvage

you are an evening in my dreams
a gentle wing across my face
there is some way I think I can
touch you or this day then I
might find you flickering in a
thought across the room or the baby

I would meet you halfway as I am
inevitable on this island of words
reflecting all things and my life

lifting my arms in some devotion
to hold you endlessly as the
cities die alone without us

I will meet you therefore
in that frame my thoughts
a crushing blow in an opera
that breaks the tension on this island
like garlic in the room . . .
paradise is like a drumbeat of blood
sounds that remind of salt.

                                        saturday sept. 27/69

capricorn

"I creep across the
stars looking for your shadow
here beside me settling with
the weather"

I have not touched
hands since october
since your silver
blouse your leather skirt

my face has not touched
water since your hair
since the blue stone
the funnel
of the earth my island

O my country
hands
my face
apart from you
landscapes from scent
what is life without
a sky to destroy?

there are people
who live in mountains
enforcing extinction
from the sun half dreams
of winter and soft snow

I am made of water
and phantoms a desperate
choice of words for love
has overruled my life tonight

I have come from the sea
to dissolve my thoughts
to roll you in salt
to shed my shadow
like the air's thin lips

I am above all reason
like a human face
like a circle
like an island of water
against mankind

it's all like christmas
this poem your profile
your eyebrows patrol my
senses like a green
language in spring

I will give you oars
my sleep the cables
of dawn   the flow of
clay too brittle to
touch permitting love

this island binds me in time
take this sea these sentences

from my belly a floating lily
above my flesh and I will fold
you like a brilliant kiss.

                                                           summer/69

Ode to Love

My island is trouble:
I have found wet grass in my armpits
and yellow paint in my navel since you left

Do you believe in a cold sane reality?
love is love like a mountain in the room
with a common cold so take my head
I am a wandering snowshoe at your feet

I cannot sleep there is sand in my shoes
there is a wine spot in my dreams that makes me dizzy
I feel like a cloud in the Pacific Ocean stunned by the weather
like an old cover on a new book in your hands
if I were a fur coat you could not get me off in case of fire
I'm interested in the finer things in life like swimming to
      Australia
in a heat wave in my arms with only salt between us
we will stop smoking for days on end in our journey
you make me restless when you use up all the air around us
I feel like a gorilla in a chocolate shower
when we watch the sun go down for the last time
if I were lost on this island I would send you my
heart on a raft with some lunch and a love letter:

            "My Dearest I am lost."

I am needed here like the sky needs air traffic therefore
I am bored with the idea of life without you on this planet
I want you to be my room deodorant my favorite stone
O ship of love I wish you would blow up when I think of

internal motivation I think of my liver on rainy days when it
   hurts
poets are really nice people they're like giant trees
full of sap!

O sun sun my life has not been a drag after all
I could have been a number in a marble game

When I think of you I can spare myself from sleep
I can be as loyal as Blue Cross and as silly as this poem
I am killing my ash tray with an overdose of butts
when I talk to my ash tray about you it gets bored
my subjects are monotonous so it tells me
That's life ash tray.

I will wrap myself in toothpaste every morning and bring
you your favorite coffee for I will be your cup
how can I become famous when I am so distracted?

There is a tiny creep in the room that steals my cigarettes
I won't kill him because I'm in love and nothing else matters
but love on this gorgeous Earth that we're on this wonderful
   trap
Anyhow I feel like an overcrowded greenhouse when you're
   around

Ode to Love—Part 2
(litany)

"I am alone in New York I am the mud
from heaven I have distracted this
society with the filth of my life
I have pumped and polluted the streets
with my determinations I have willed
my will with a monotonous infamy
Destroy yourself if you don't know!
I speak from a terrible inner pace
before the beginning of my birth
I have been the unnatural vigor of
dreams the meditations of the insane
and the model of the dead my dreams
are countries in another city in hotels
with solitary radios with eyelids and
lipstick on the thread of life for a
dollar I have slaughtered my loins for
a fake and for the scandal in my body
in pursuit of love and my life I take
this for myself with no qualms with no
discretion for I do not fear my blood
any longer or the minerals in my body
before an instant death surrounded by
criticism and chaos waiting for a final
star in a room for a glittering tear on
the floor the color of heaven for I have
been my own somnambulist saint the invention
of my nerves love has been a temporary lift
from nostrils and navel-sucking and from the
petty boredom of a hot body around the channels
of my waist in some emergency!"   O fuck who cares.

But it is Sunday and I have come through without a scratch
or a watch to tell you of that time or anyone for that
matter my excitement is your short black hair lighting your
cigarettes over a dinner table or holding your hand in the
theater or saying nothing when we're together on an island
on a magic ocean in the mornings.

This is what I have my new life and a beach full of cabbage
so we can be alone in this mad world of silly images I
promise you 80 years more of life because I feel like a
watermelon covered with Jergens Lotion!   I am mad to think
these things but it is a good and kindly madness that will
do the world some good.

I have lived with a broken heart since I can remember since
Webster wrote his wonderful book to Mary if I stop writing
I'll go out like a light and wake up in another marathon
or another life dreaming of you I need coffee.
Someone has put a hand in my coffee if it were yours I don't
think I would stir it for fear of dying of my own perspiration
if you suddenly appeared in my room nude how would you go back
if I drank the coffee? That's life baby.

Men cry because they do not have the will to live I wonder if
living is a sideline if you're not in love? I wonder about a
lot of things like how you take a shower how you grin when you
brush your teeth how you feel when you think of me as the only
man in the world like me?

Well the time has come to clip my nails and play one last

piece and settle with the Earth for a night and a token of
love your love and the nourishment of a dream with you your
eyes like growing flowers your flowers the vegetations of
Spain a great sadness if you will it on the world.

sunday, sept. 7/69

yellow

sara

1

in the morning I sit up and wonder
where I left my hat in envy
sins are monotonous soft and easy
but I lament for an eternal omen:
to split my lip when I kiss you

2

I have fallen to earth
have you noticed I tremble
when you walk across the room
because my wounds are mysterious
like clear insanity I want to touch
your hair and tell you of my rash
and the endless sparrows when my
voice travels to you.

tuesday, feb. 3/70
east 5th street

canto

sara

1
below—
the two of us

2
the snow takes us through the snow
and we are spotless

> wednesday, feb. 3/70
> east 5th street

sara

9:30

I
love
you
because

I
love
spoons

may 14/70

june sara

O white new york
a yellow cab
of sun and you
in my pants like
a million subways . . .

things will be all right although
i have brushed my teeth for both
of us this morning i always dream
of mice of lettuce red
cellophane wonderful garlic
mysterious bathrooms beautiful
women long legs the oracles of
the earth thick with snow

it is the sun in your purple eyes
or the head of a day in june
after we fight i feel horrible
i see sun spots marching in the
shower because i am a genius
now that we are swimming in coffee
and full of politeness let's fuck

        you are an insect with
        four legs clouds over a
        river and gentle water
        i am two of your legs
        and who knows what
        goes by

below.

                                                       june 9/70
                                                       east 5th street

my life

sara

1
my life is
a sailor's
face

everything
flows

so crush me
between your
pliers

I will
ease your
swallowing

2
I am a truck
here are the
footprints

you're
flying south
on my waist

another word
for atmosphere

in which
I move.

june 29/70
east 5th street

river	**sara**
I am furious like a city of rumors	I move over your birth and breathe deeply
I look at my feet and see children	
O sun O sun	I love the world and feel your touch
I have put light ning thru my hands	
whoever finds me will be beautiful	I pray to animals and flee
I will be plentiful like the rocks	I linger above you and smell
to see my father nude discover our fingers	I must put my self

the avalanche
between us
my pure figure

image of life
adore me!
adore me!

out
early

with
your
finger

and lean
my elbows
over you.

july 6/70
east 5th street

morning sara

toward the end you are sunburned
and I am a blister if only I weren't
human I would throw you out with
great passion no excuses just love
for your own good—

you shit!   you're late!

since I have nothing better to do
let me watch you piss and I will
excuse you from the world
call you lake or long-leg-waterfall
I am hungry and go thru your underwear

give me some hot soup or
I'll suck on the curtains!

would you like an omelette
with diced candles and mushrooms?
or a garbage truck in an opera?
do you put lipstick on your nipples?
I'd like to think so your body like
the streets in Amsterdam the harbor
in your hair the canals down your
back in the mornings as I sweep the
flowers off you when the alarm goes
off I wake up like a net fumbling for love

so pull me close to you
and strike the morning ice
and I will gather myself up

from the filth of dreams
shave shower and kiss you!

>	july 7/70
>	east 5th street

The Author

FRANK LIMA was born in New York of Mexican parents in 1939. He attended New York City public schools, and is currently an addiction specialist with the Hispanic Association for a Drug-free Society. In 1962 he won the Gotham Book Mart Avant-garde Poetry Prize at the Wagner College Literary Conference. He has had several grants from the Poets Foundation, and a selection of his work, *Inventory,* was published in a limited edition by the Tibor De Nagy Gallery in 1964. The same year he won the John Hay Whitney Award. He has been anthologized in John Bernard Myers' *The Poets of New York* and in the *Anthology of New York Poets* edited by David Shapiro and Ron Padgett. His poems have also appeared in *Evergreen Review, Floating Bear, Paris Review, Angel Hair, Mother, Cornu Emplumado, Signal,* and *Audit.* He has two daughters and lives on 2nd Avenue in New York with his wife Sara.

"One decade of Suffering City Withdrawal Pains is focused here in the few poems a young man finds in his head by Art Miracle and offers Futurity, a little Free Joy from Frank Lima."

—Allen Ginsberg

FRANK LIMA was born in New York of Mexican parents in 1939. He attended New York City public schools. At present he is an addiction specialist with the Hispanic Association for a Drug-free Society. In 1962 he won the Gotham Book Mart Avant-garde Poetry Prize at the Wagner College Literary Conference. His poems have appeared in a number of magazines, reviews, and anthologies. He has two daughters and lives on 2nd Avenue in New York with his wife Sara.

$2.95

0-325-04650-X